The Hospital

General Editor : HENRY PLUCKROSE

Text by FRANK PEACOCK

Photographs by G. W. HALES

FRANKLIN WATTS
LONDON

Words about a Hospital

accidents
ambulance
anaesthetic

bandages
bed
better
blood pressure

care
changes
charge
children
clean
cleaners
cook
curtains

doctors
drawn
dressings
drivers

fathers
feel

games
germs

happy
heavy
help
hospital
hurt

ill
injection

jobs

lies
lift

masks
meals
medicines
models
mothers

nurses

operations
outdoors

perform
photographs
play
playroom
porters
prescribe
pulse

radiographer
rest
road
room

separate
serve
short
sick
sleep
surgeons

temperature
tests
thermometer
times
tired
treatment

useful

visitors

wakes
ward
ward sister
watch
weights
wrist
wrong

X-ray

Grateful thanks are due to the National Association for the Welfare of Children in Hospital for help in preparing the text of this book and in supplying some of the photographs. Thanks are also due to Dr. Harvey, St. Charles' Hospital, London W.10, for kind permission to take photographs at the hospital.

Franklin Watts Limited,
8 Cork Street,
London, W.1.

Copyright 1976 © Franklin Watts Limited
Reprinted 1976, 1978, 1979

SBN 85166 578 0

Printed in Great Britain by
Tindal Press, Chelmsford, Essex

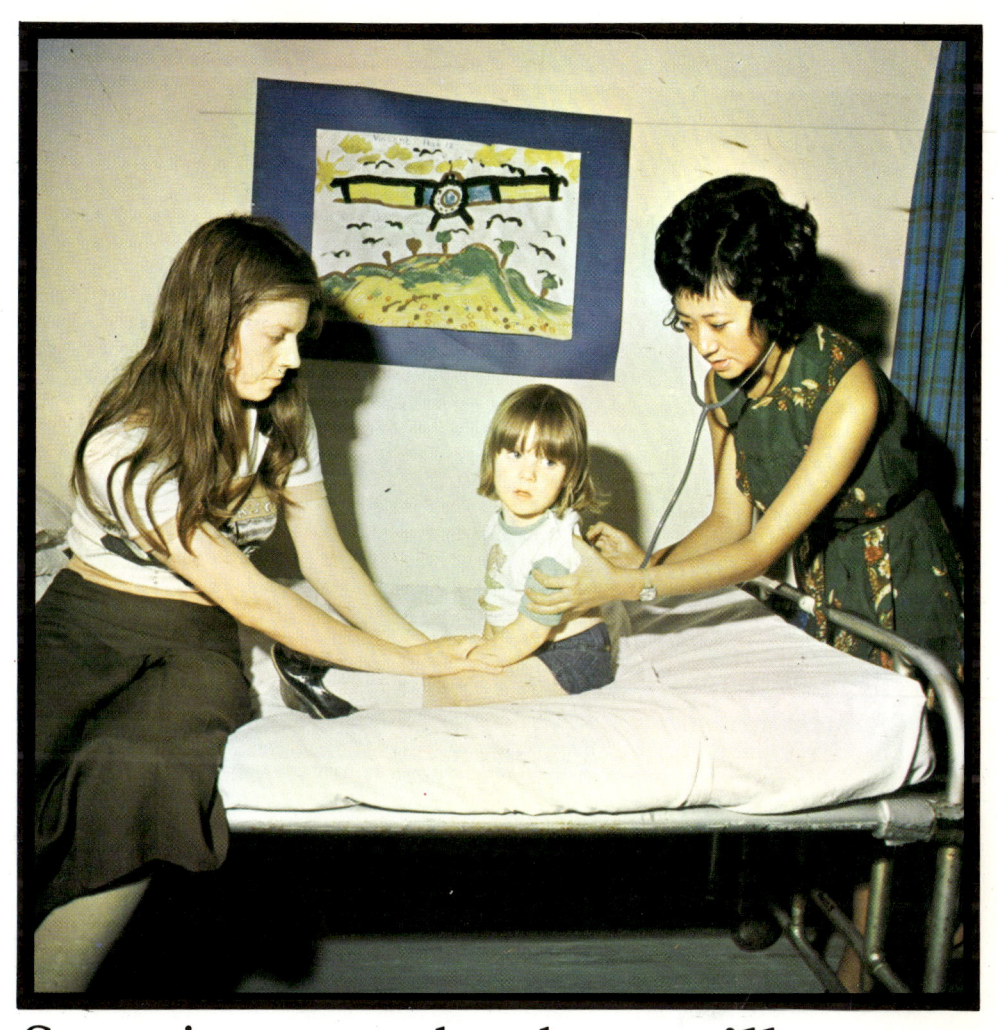

Sometimes people who are **ill**
have to go to **hospital**
to get **better.**
Doctors will **help** them to get better.

Some people have to go to hospital
in an **ambulance.**
Ambulances help at **accidents**
at home, at work, or on the **road.**

Ambulance men are very good **drivers.**
They also know how to take **care** of
sick people.

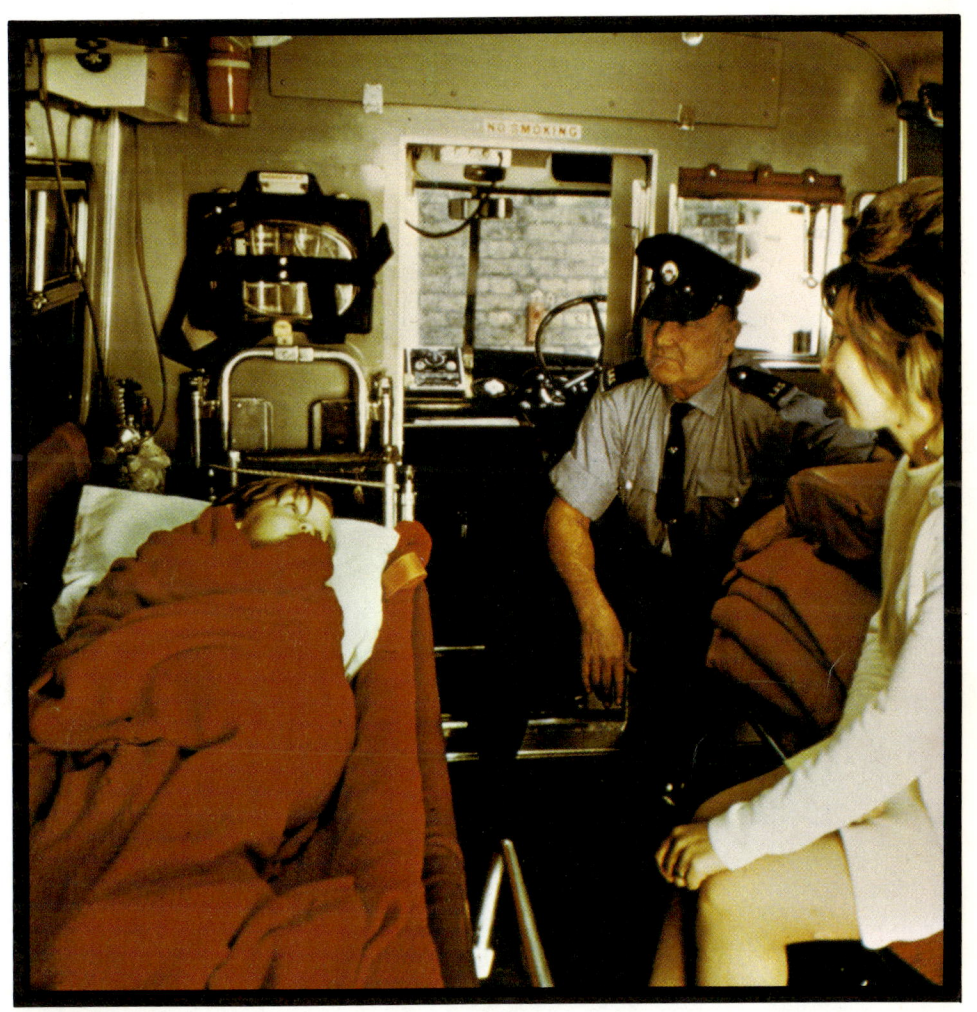

Sometimes a sick person **lies**
in a **bed** in a **ward.**
There are several beds in a ward.
Curtains can be **drawn** round each bed.

Sometimes a sick person lies in a bed
in a **separate room.**
Visitors come to the wards
as well as to the rooms.

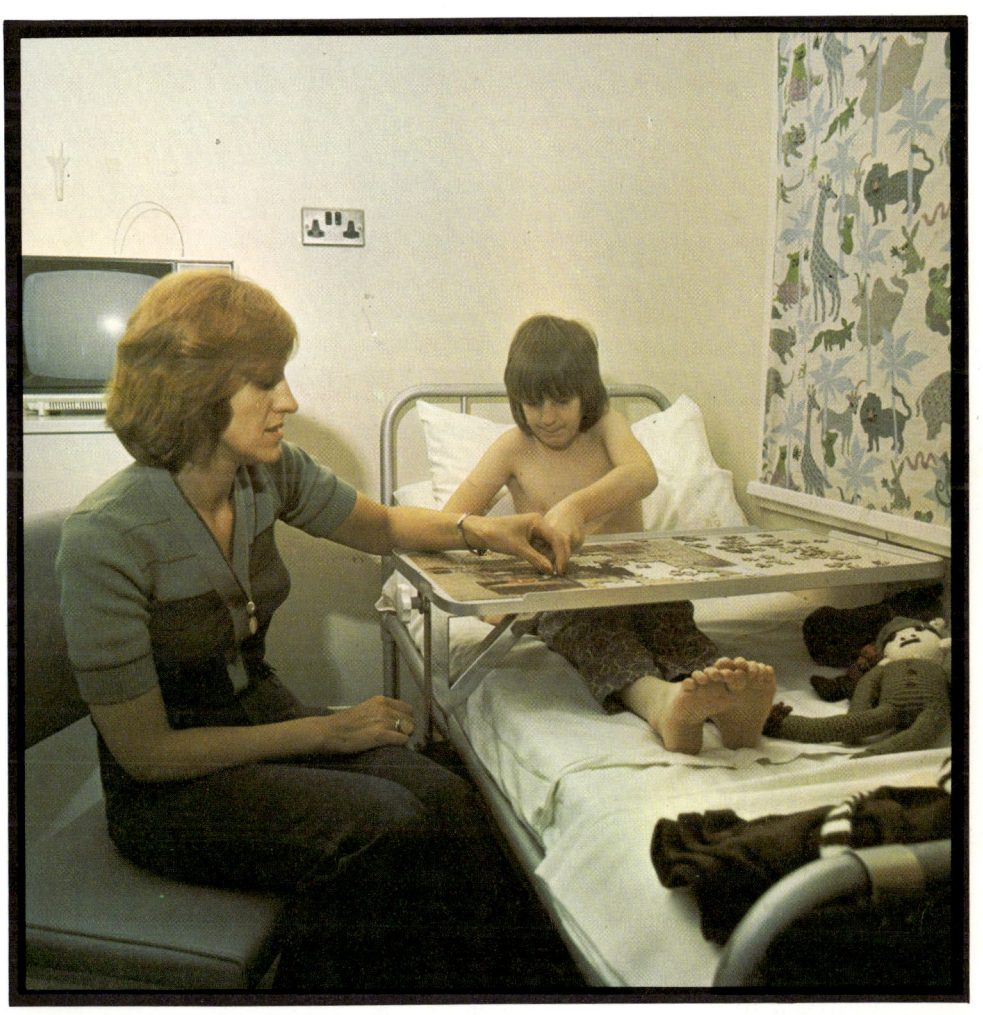

In hospital there are always
nurses to help.
Nurses help patients in many ways.

Nurses give the sick people
the **medicines**
that the doctors **prescribe.**

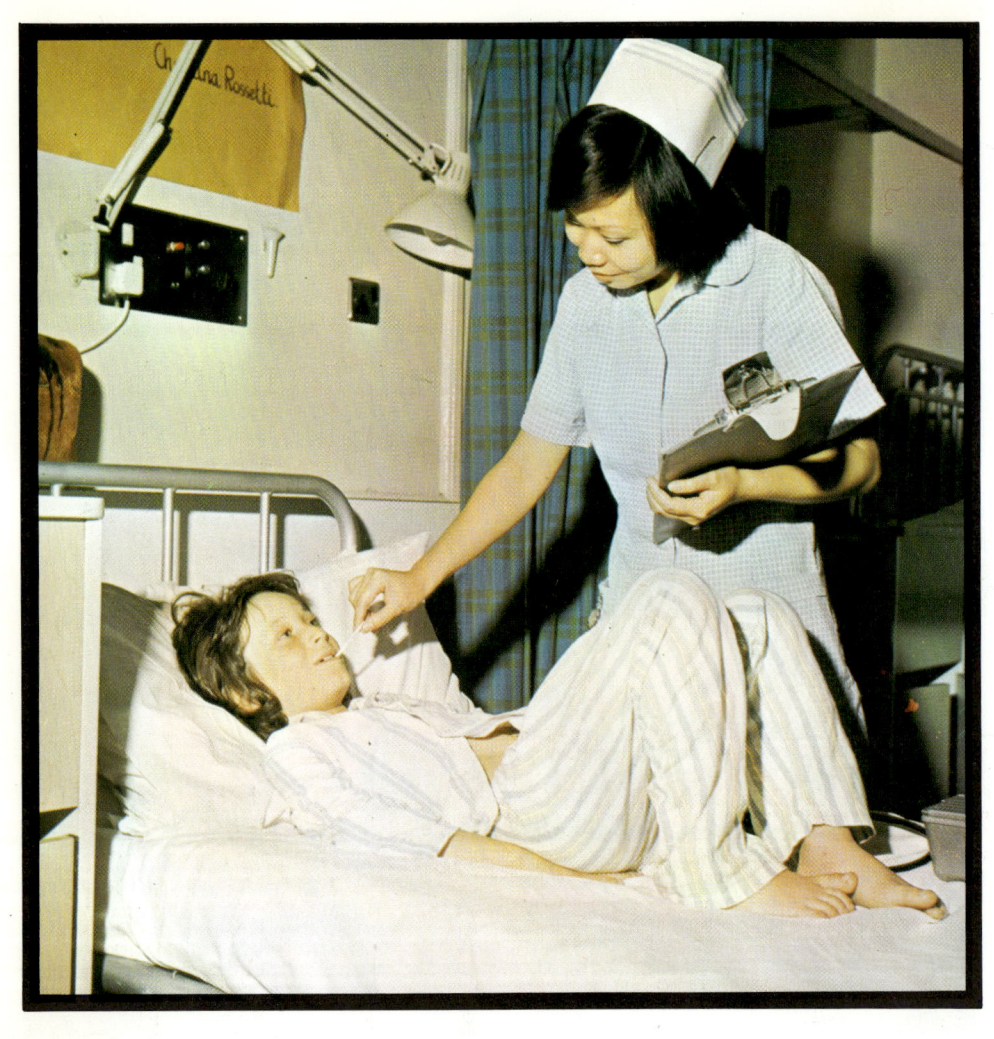

A nurse takes
a boy's **temperature**.
She uses a **thermometer**.

A nurse takes a boy's **pulse.**

She can **feel** the pulse in his **wrist.**

She **times** the pulse with her **watch.**

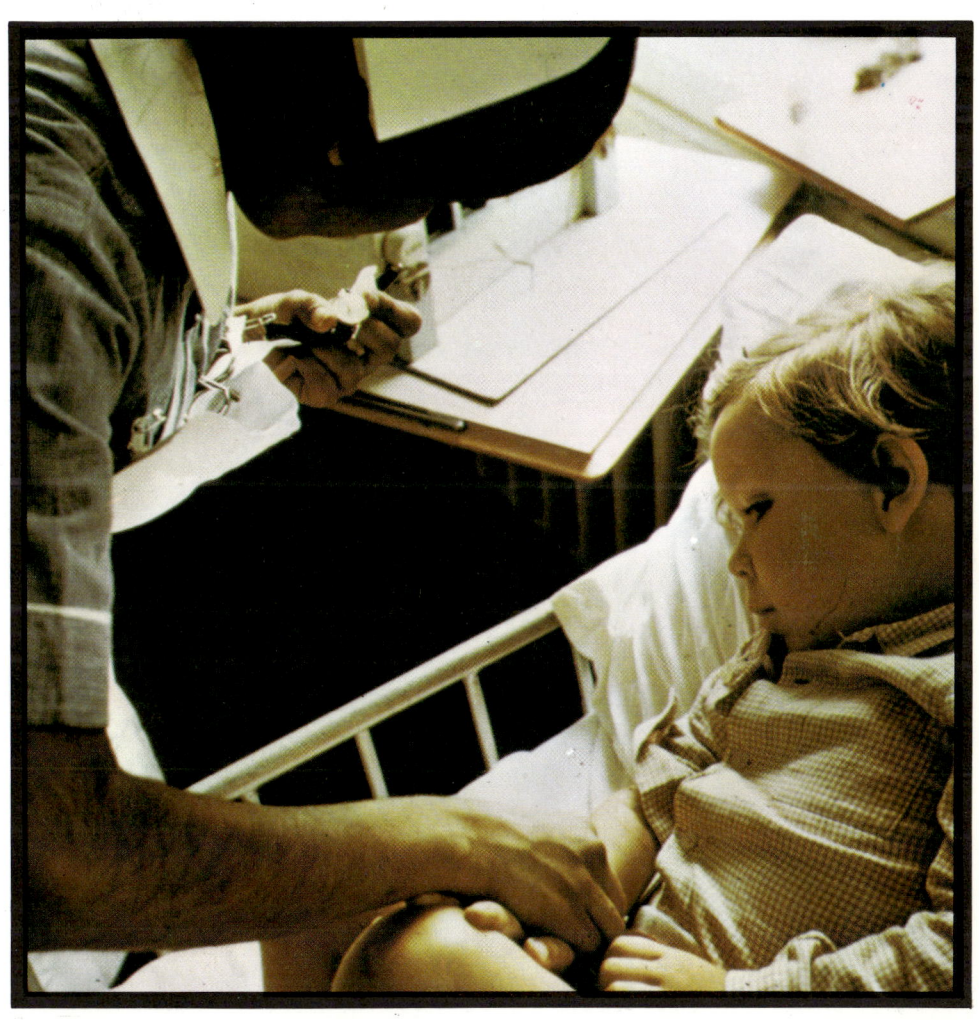

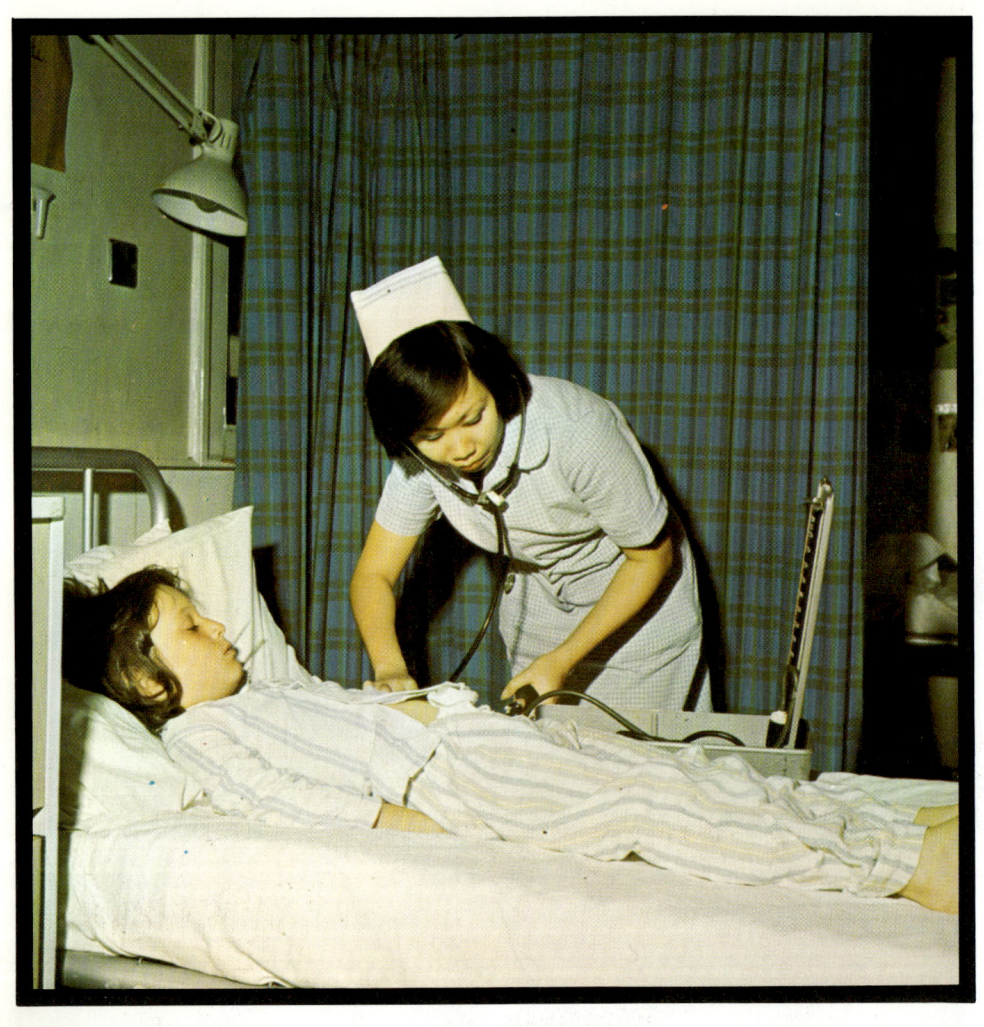

A nurse takes
  a boy's **blood pressure.**
This helps the doctor
  to find out if anything is **wrong.**

A nurse **changes bandages** and **dressings.**

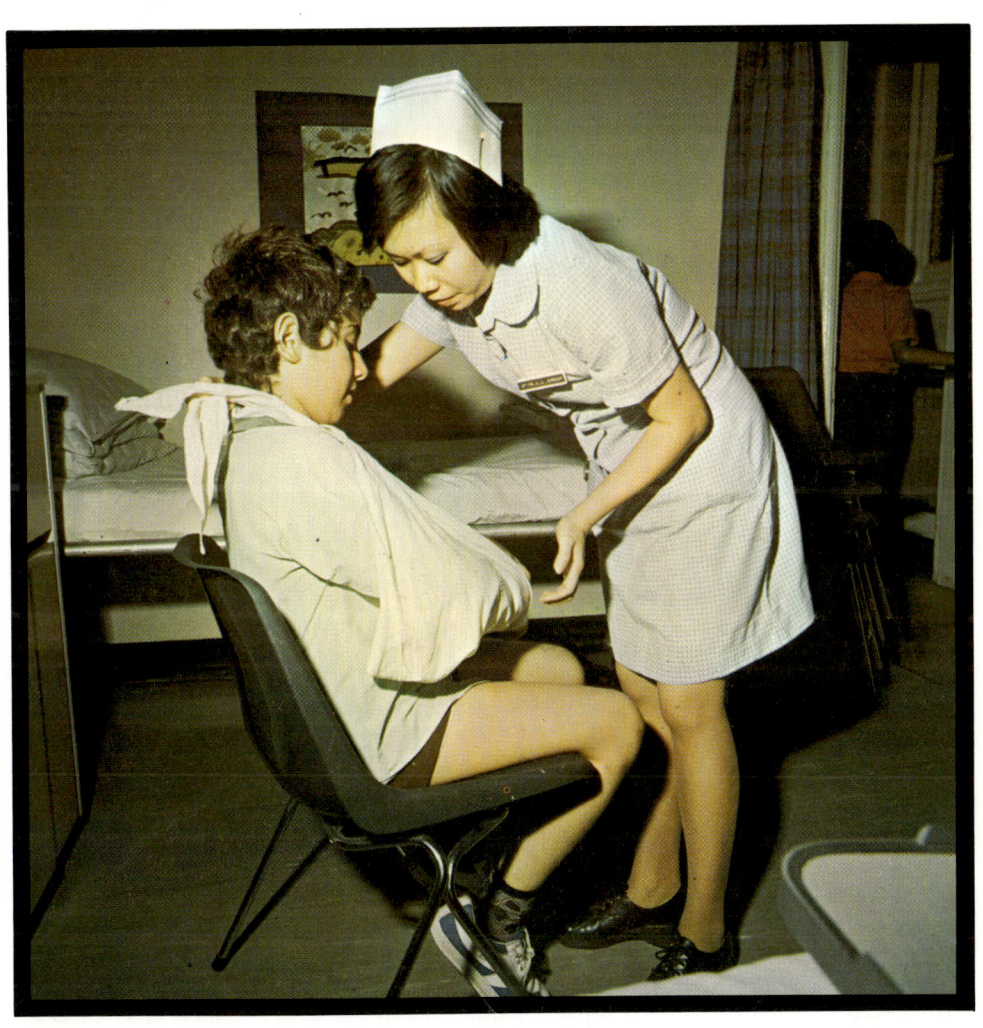

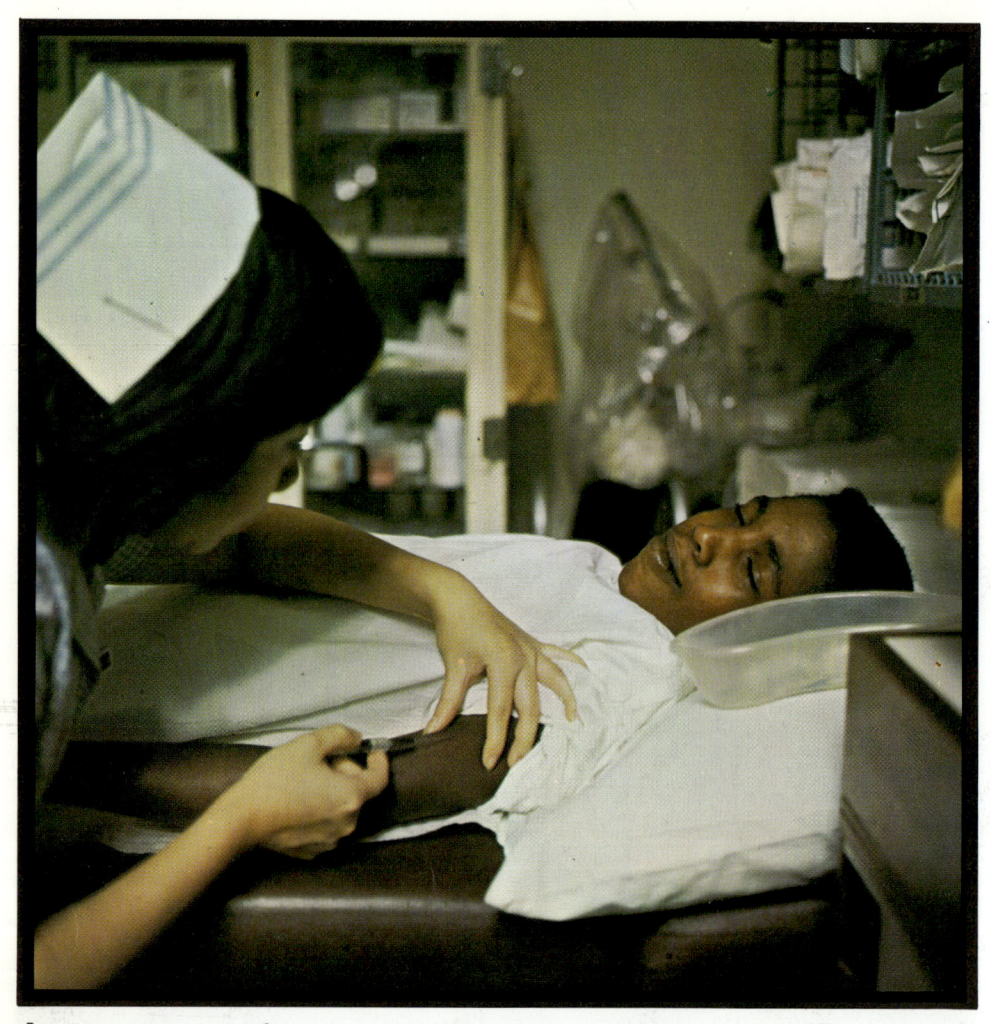

A nurse gives an **injection.**

It may **hurt,** but only for a very

short time.

It will help to make the person better.

The **ward sister** is in **charge** of all the nurses in a ward.

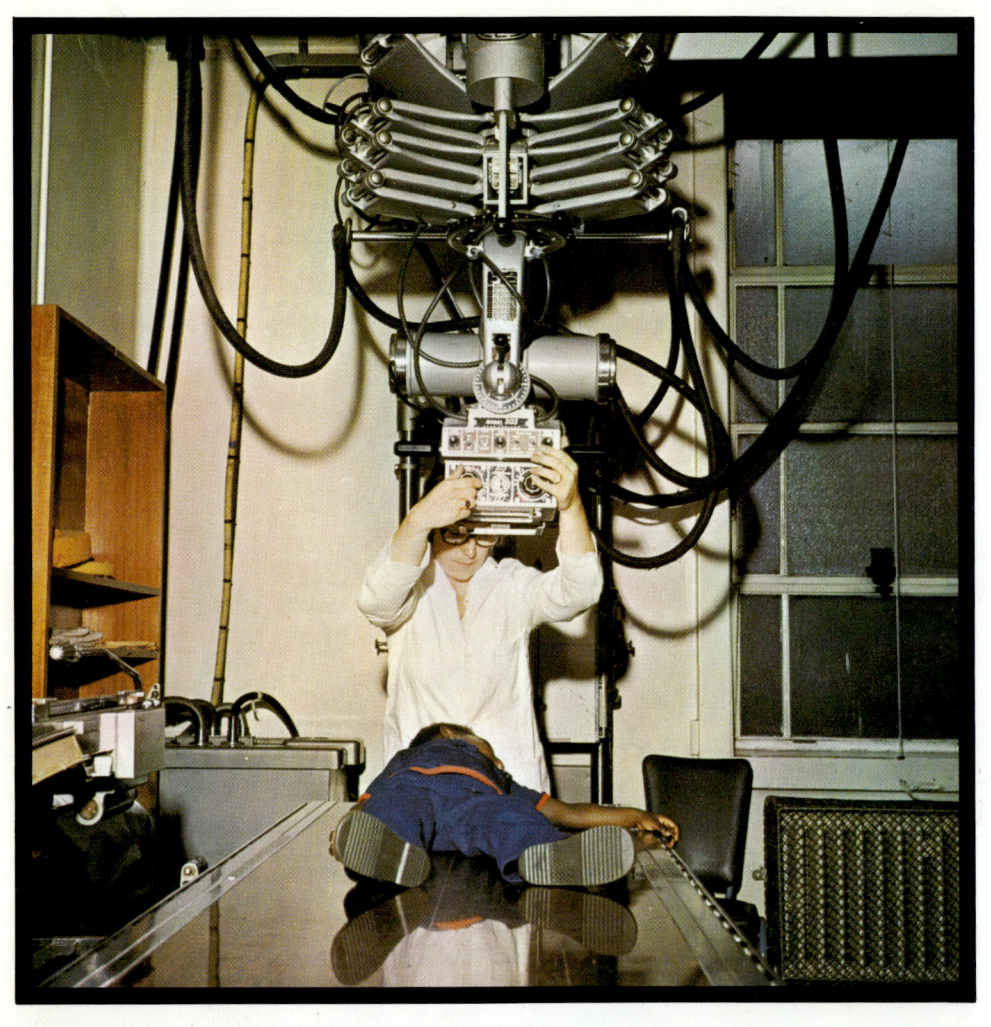

In hospital a sick person can have
special **tests** and **treatment**.
The **radiographer** takes
special **X-ray photographs**.

X-ray photographs
   can help the doctor find out
   if anything is wrong with the
   sick person.

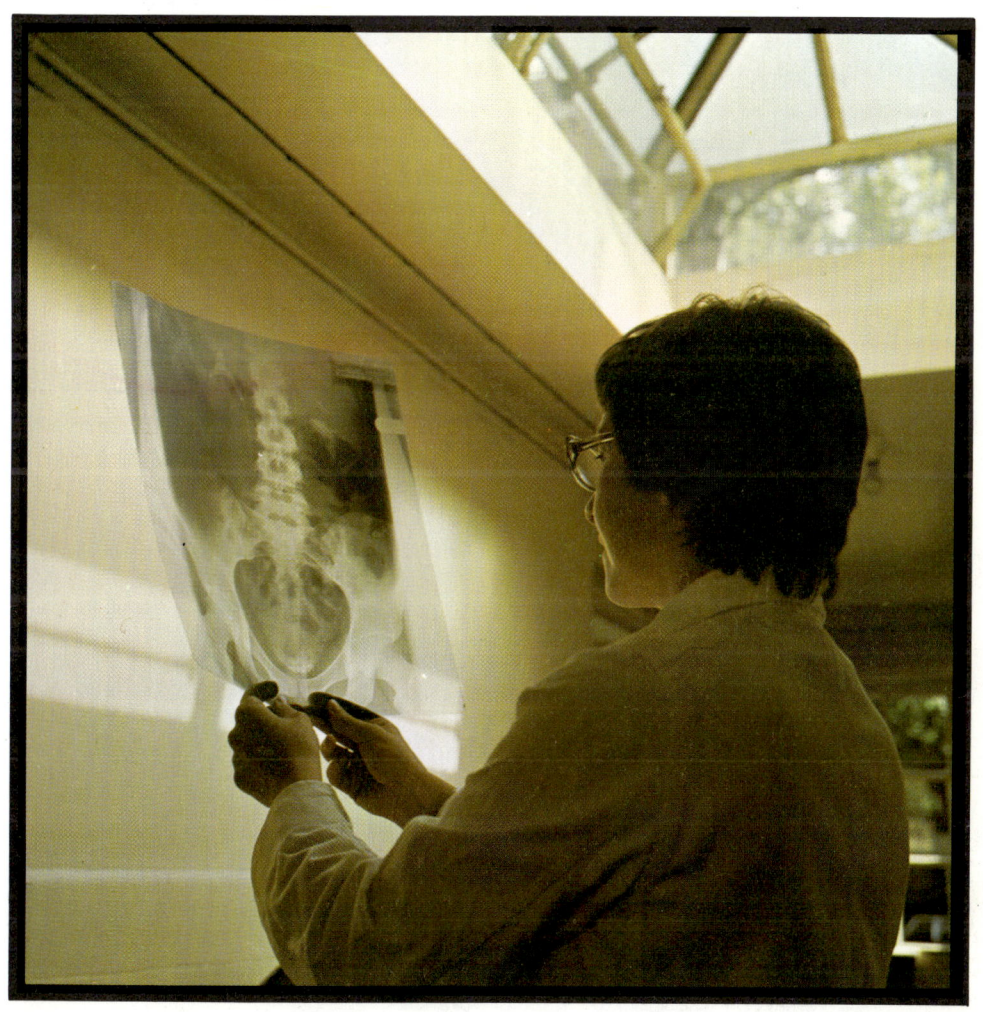

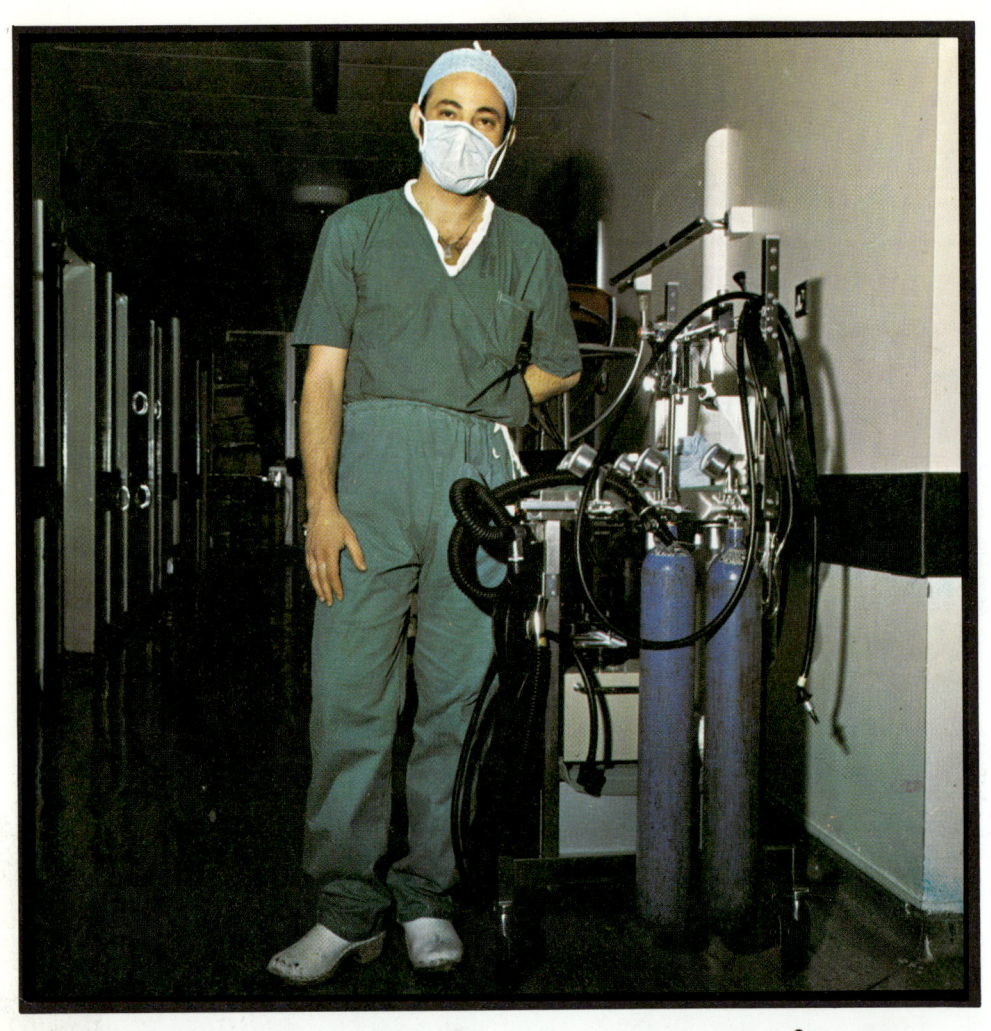

Surgeons perform operations
on sick people who need them.
They wear **masks** to keep **germs**
away from the sick people.

Before an operation
    a sick person is given an injection
    and then an **anaesthetic**
    to make him have a special **sleep.**

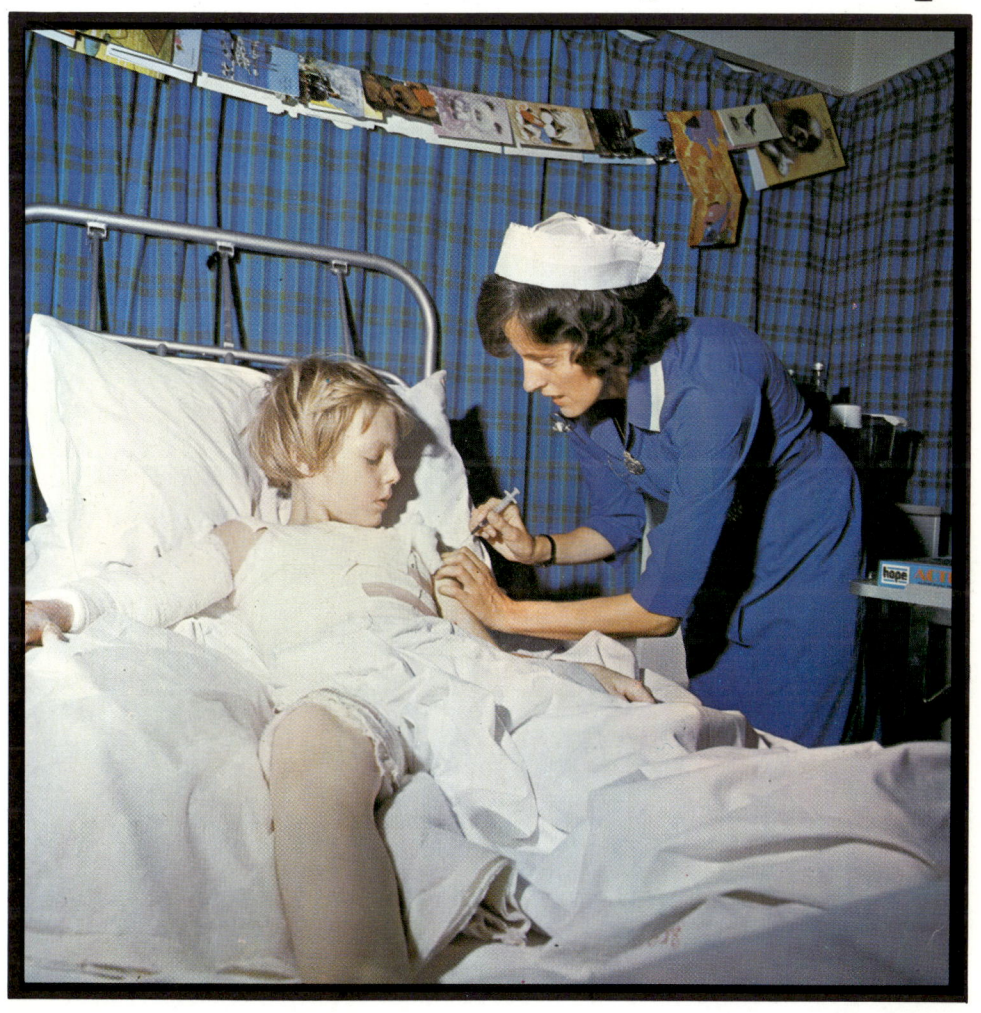

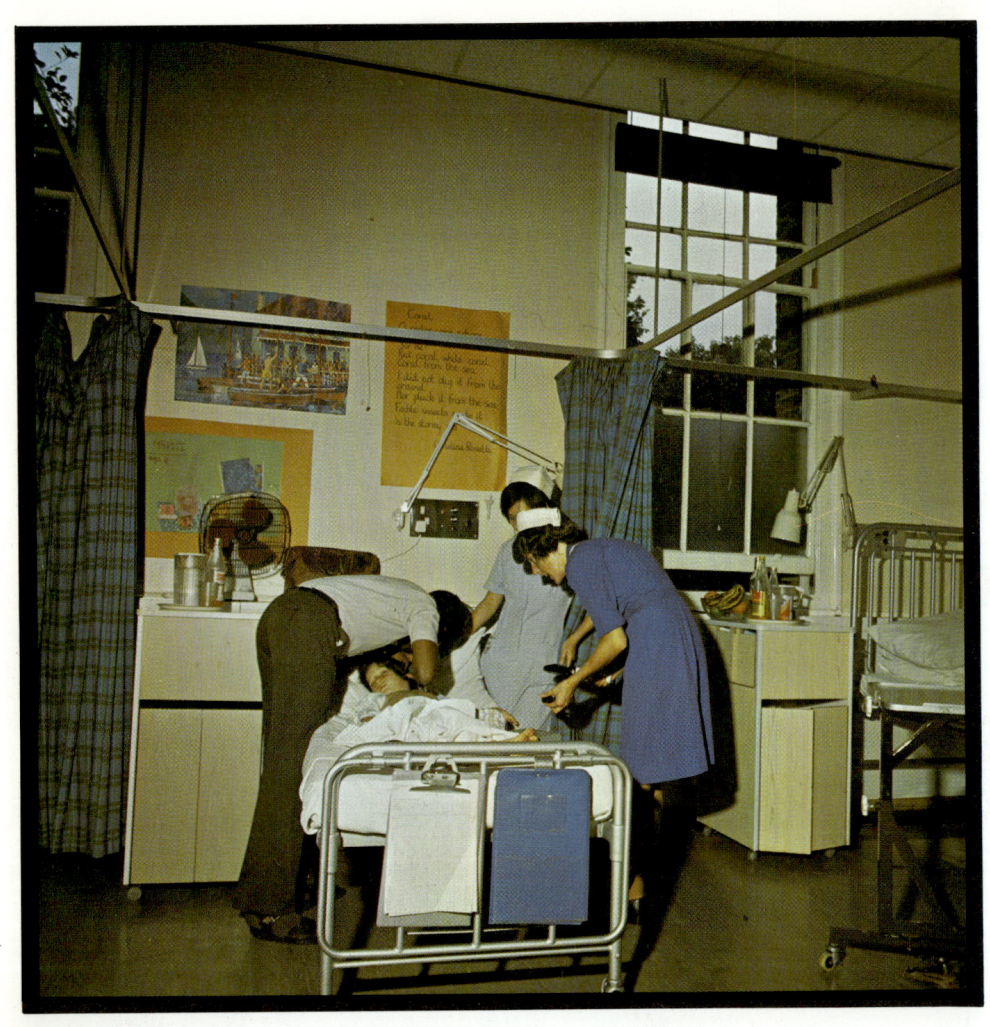

When the sick person **wakes** up
   after the operation, he is very **tired**.
He needs **rest** and special care
   to get better quickly.

Children in hospital
are looked after
by a special children's doctor.

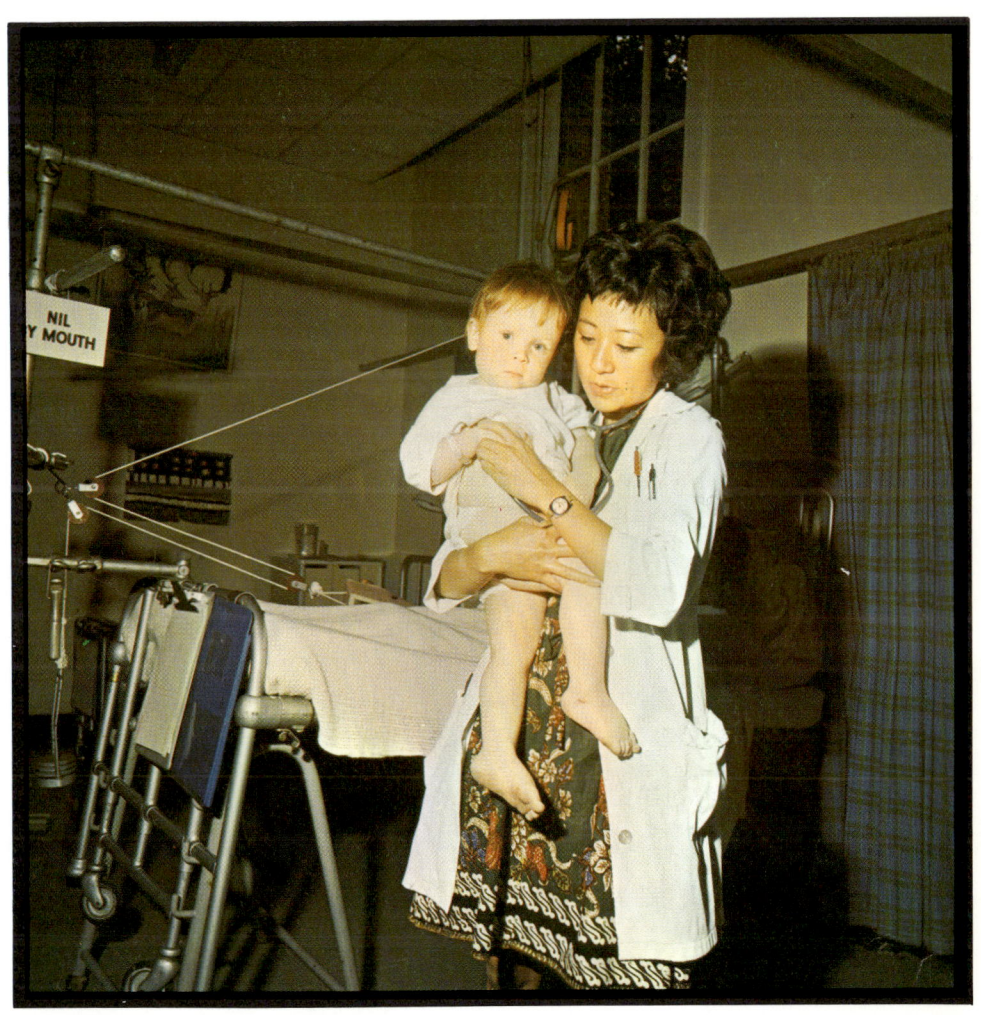

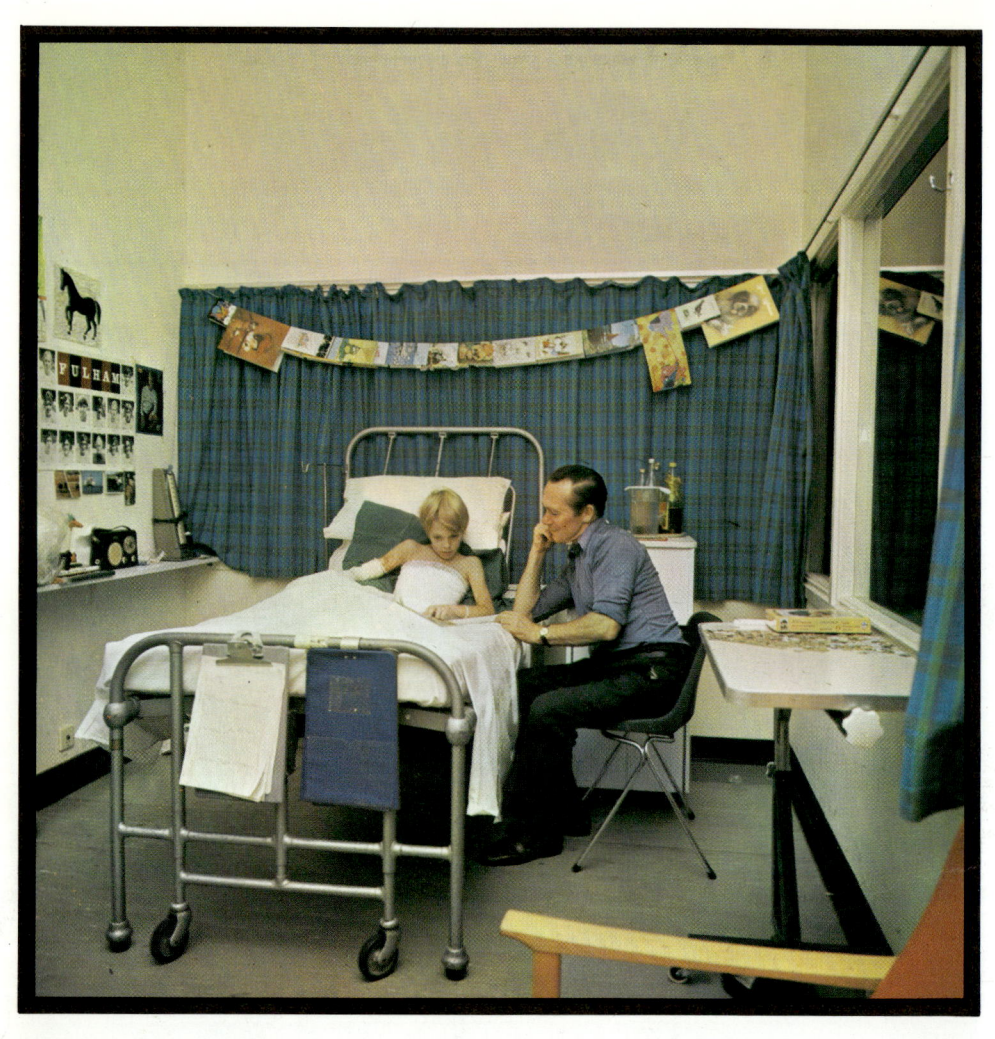

Mothers and **fathers** come
to visit children in hospital.

Sometimes the mother can live
at the hospital
while her child is there.

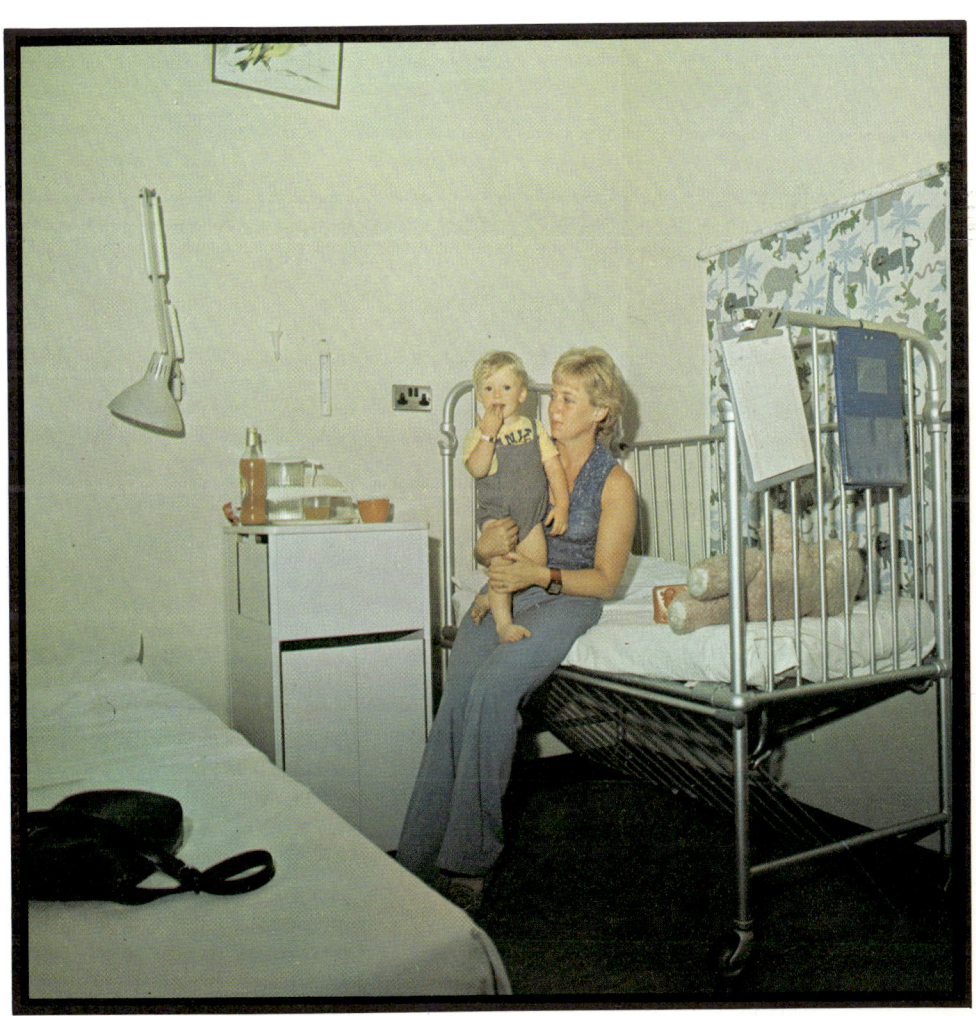

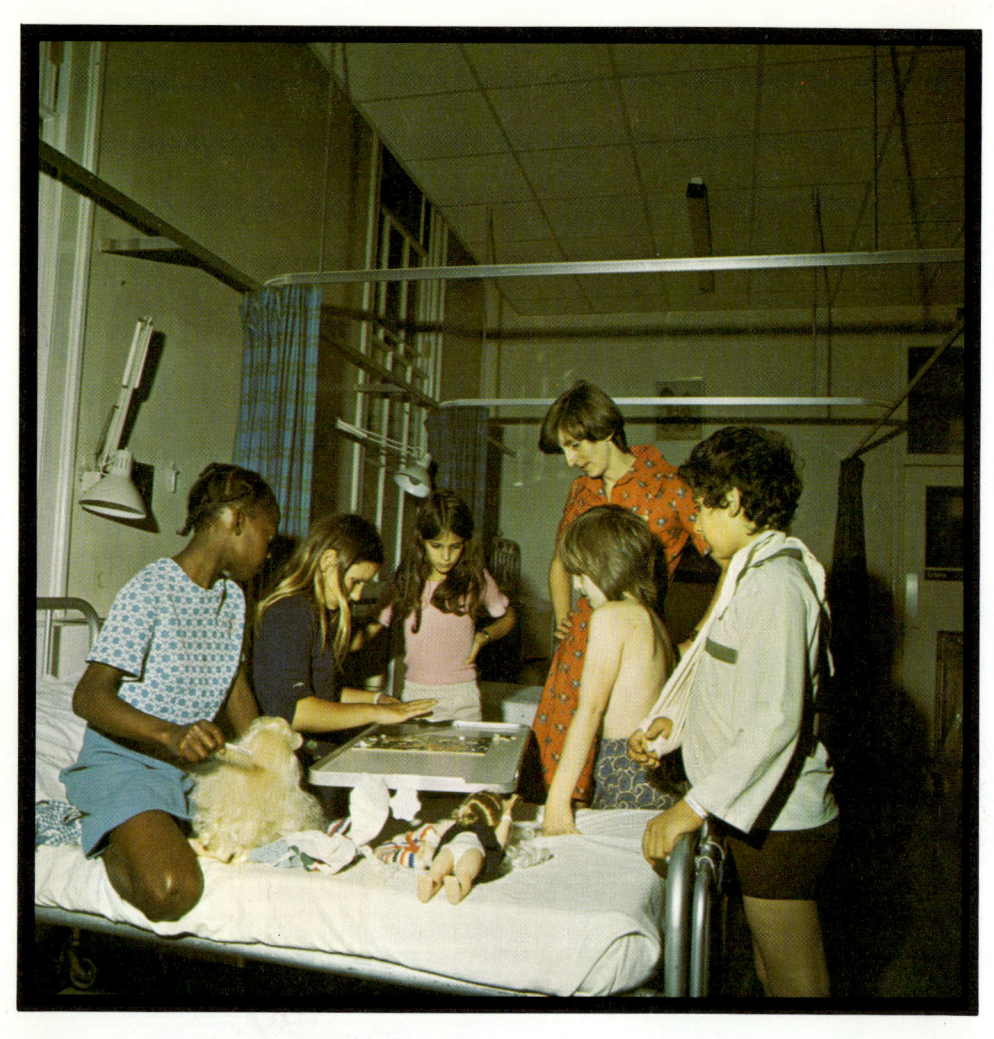

Children in hospital
can **play games**
and make **models** in the ward.

When they are well enough,
children in hospital
can play games and make models
in a special **playroom.**

When they are well enough,
children in hospital
can play **outdoors.**

People come to the hospital
   to help the nurses.
They play games with the children.

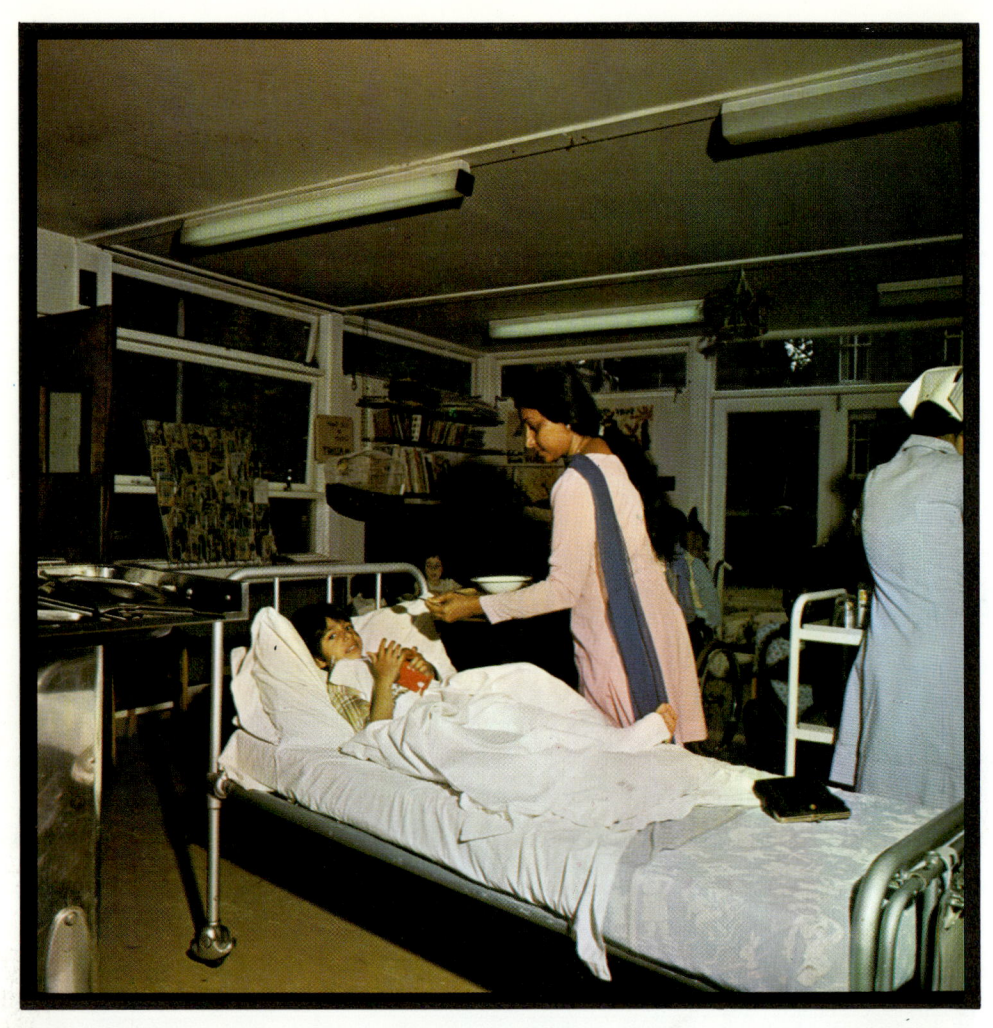

People come to the hospital and help
to **serve** the **meals** to patients in bed.
If they are well enough, patients
can eat their meals out of bed.

Some people working at the
hospital **cook** the meals.
Others help to serve the meals.

A hospital must be kept **clean.**
The **cleaners** come to work
every day.

Porters in a hospital
do many **useful jobs.**
They help to **lift heavy weights.**

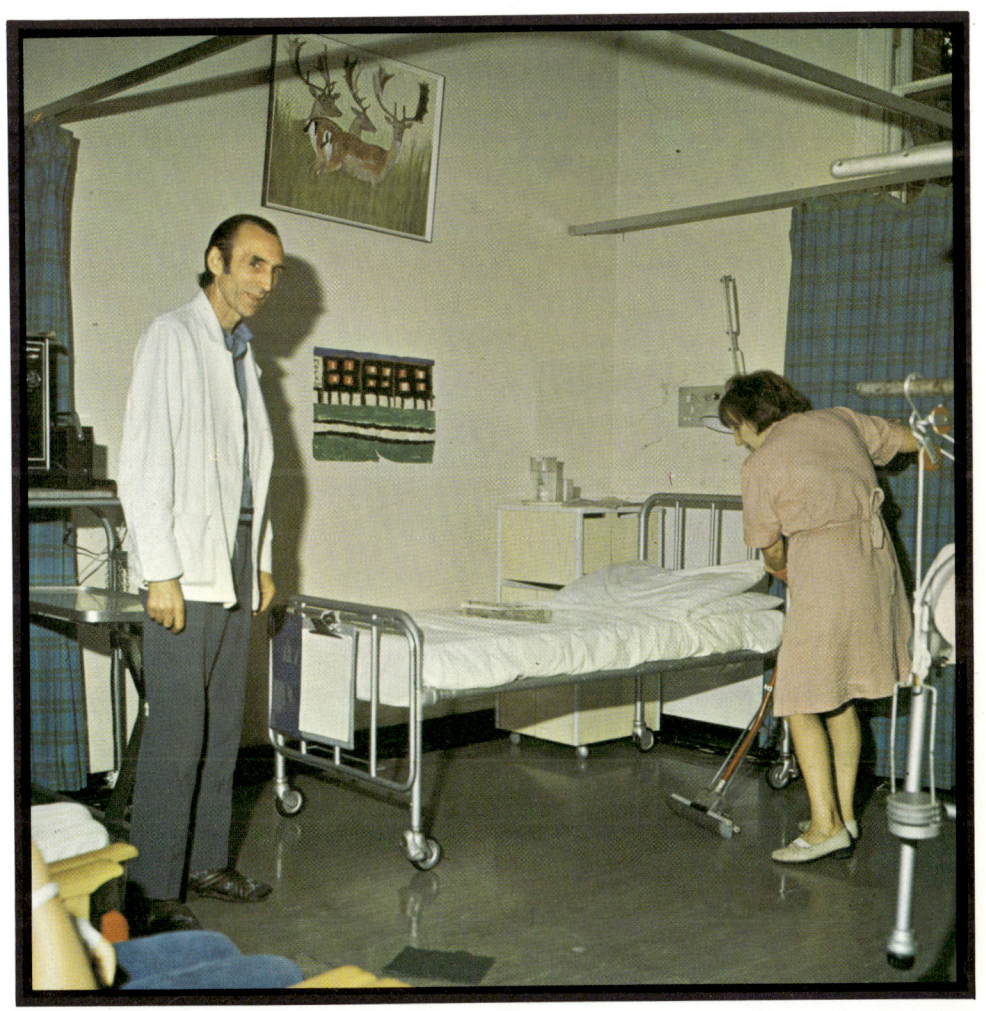

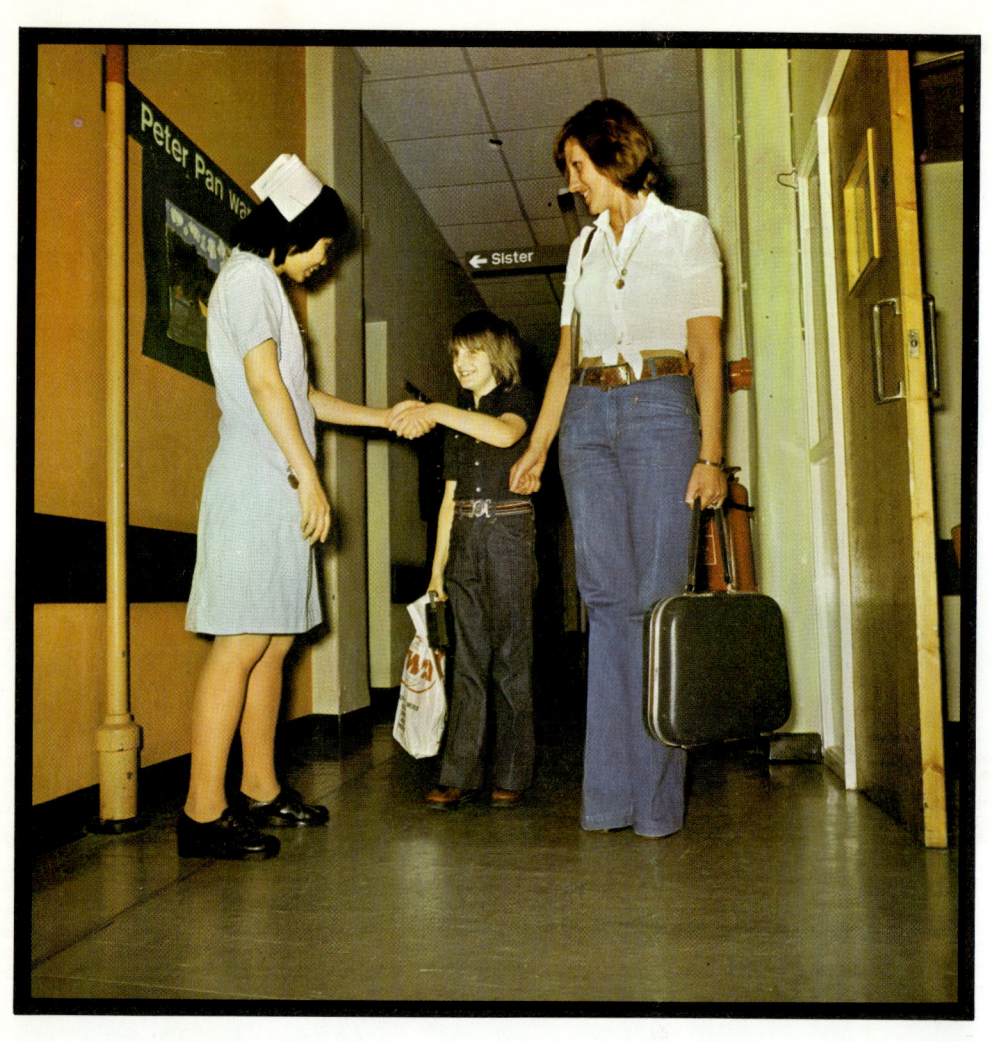

It is a **happy** time
   when sick people are well enough
   to leave hospital and go home.